AMERICAN INDIANS

Curator of North ... History

This book ... the Iroc ...

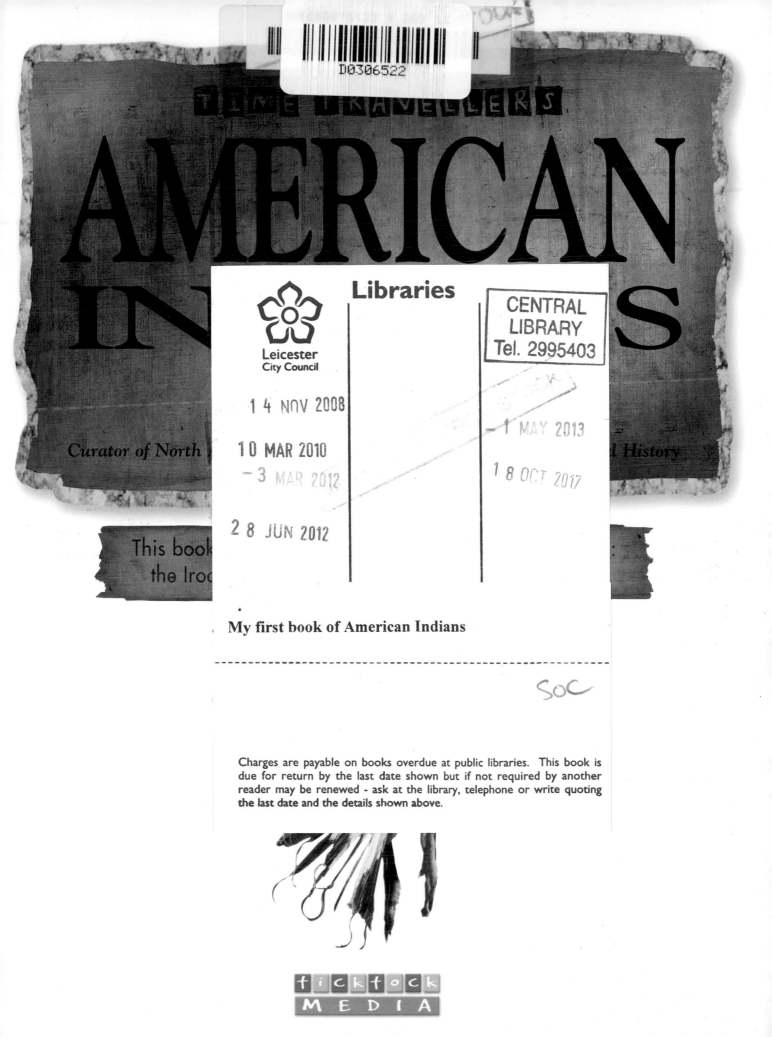

ticktock
MEDIA

Copyright © ticktock Entertainment Ltd 2004
First published in Great Britain in 2005 by ticktock Media Ltd.,
Unit 2, Orchard Business Centre, North Farm Road, Tunbridge Wells, Kent TN2 3XF

ISBN 1 86007 612 2 pbk
Printed in China

A CIP catalogue record for this book is available from the British Library.

Picture credits (t=top; b=bottom; c=centre; l=left; r=right): Alamy: 11l, 17cr. Courtesy of the Division of Anthropology, American Museum of
Natural History: 9tr (artefact catalogue number 50/6525AB), 9cr (50/6492), 9br (1/4965), 11br (10/24), 13tr (50/7267), 13cr (50/7268),
13br (501/5622), 17br (50/4362), 23cr (50/9404). British Museum: 10. Corbis: 2-3, 4bl, 5, 6-7, 8, 12, 13l, 15r, 16, 18, 19, 21, 22, 23l,
23br. G. Peter Jemison: 11tr. North Wind Picture Archives: 9tl. Susanne Page: 20-21 (main). Smithsonian Institute: 17l. Woolaroc Museum,
Bartlesville, Oklahoma: 14-15. Every effort has been made to trace the copyright holders and we apologise in advance for any unintentional
omissions. We would be pleased to insert the appropriate acknowledgement in any subsequent edition of this publication.

Contents

Glossary

On page 24 there is a glossary of
words and terms. The glossary words
appear in **bold** in the text.

3

Spreading across the land

The first Americans came from Asia and settled in North America between 60,000 and 12,000 years ago.

These peoples spread across North America in small groups. Some settled in the forests of the northeast, others in the far north where it is cold.

This Sioux man is wearing a traditional headdress.

Some peoples chose to live in the southeast, where it is warm all year round. Others settled in the hot deserts of the southwest.

Because each **environment** was different, the people developed their own ways of finding food, building houses, making clothes and giving thanks to the **spirits**.

BLACKFOOT

SUBARCTIC

NORTHWEST COAST

HAIDA

KWAKWAKA'WAKW

PLATEAU

FLATHEAD
NEZ PERCE

CALIFORNIA

SHOSHONI

POMO

GREAT BASIN

YOKUTS

CHUMASH

NAVAJO
HOPI
PUEBLO
APACHE

SOUTHWEST

4

Over thousands of years,
the people became hundreds of
different Native American nations,
each with their own **culture**.

The first Americans

MAP OF NORTH AMERICA

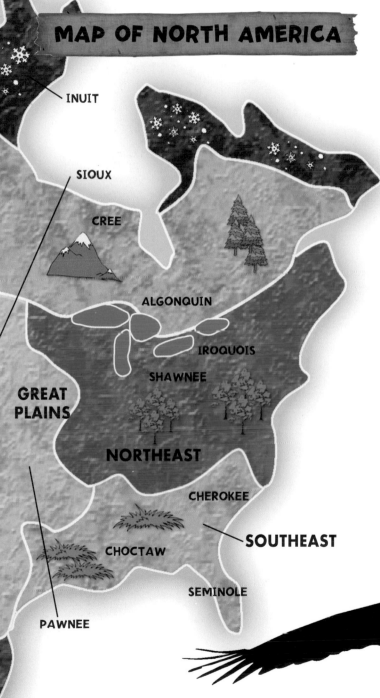

INUIT

SIOUX

CREE

ALGONQUIN

IROQUOIS

SHAWNEE

**GREAT
PLAINS**

NORTHEAST

CHEROKEE

SOUTHEAST

CHOCTAW

SEMINOLE

PAWNEE

*This map shows the homelands of some of the
Native American nations and the different
environments of North America.*

As they travelled across
the land, native people
made drawings on rocks
and in caves. The drawings
are called PETROGLYPHS.

The EAGLE is a symbol
of strength and courage
to many Native
Americans.

Important lessons

Long ago, Native Americans did not have a written language. It was very important to LISTEN AND TO REMEMBER. Children didn't go to school, but learned by watching and copying grown-ups.

Children learned **origin stories** and **legends** from listening to **storytellers**. Each part of the country had its own special stories.

A ceremonial dance at a pow-wow.

Boys began to hunt and fish with the men when they were ten years old. Some boys learned how to grow corn and other crops.

Girls helped the women. They cared for younger brothers and sisters and collected moss and furry seed heads as nappy material to put inside babies' **cradleboards**.

A Navajo woman with a baby in a cradleboard.

Children still learn tribal **traditions** from grown-ups today. This picture shows families at a **pow-wow**. These gatherings of many different tribes are held every year.

Different cultures

War bonnets were worn by GREAT PLAINS warriors. Each feather represented a brave deed.

Tribes of the northwest coast carved stories on wooden TOTEM POLES.

People of the longhouse

Tribes of the Iroquois settled in the forests of the northeast. These tribes included the Mohawk, Oneida, Onondaga, Cayuga, Seneca and Tuscarora.

The Iroquois lived in wooden longhouses, made from a frame of young trees covered with elm bark.

An Iroquois man stands alongside the reconstruction of a longhouse.

Each longhouse was home to ten or more families from the same family group, or **clan**. Bear, Turtle, Beaver and Deer are some Iroquois clan names.

8

Inside a longhouse, fires for cooking and heating divided the families' living space. Above each fire was a smoke hole in the roof.

This woodcut picture shows Iroquois families harvesting corn.

The Iroquois planted large gardens of corn, beans and squash. The beans climbed up the corn stalks and squash grew around the bottom. This arrangement was called the *Three Sisters*.

Iroquois artefacts

MUSIC was made using drums and rattles.

This Iroquois **RATTLE** is made from a turtle shell filled with pebbles.

This Iroquois **WAR CLUB** is carved from wood.

The Iroquois Confederacy

The Iroquois tribes had a long history of fighting with one another. About 1000 years ago, five Iroquois tribes formed a special group called THE IROQUOIS CONFEDERACY.

The Mohawk, Oneida, Onondaga, Cayuga and Seneca tribes agreed to live in peace under one imaginary longhouse that stretched across their **territory**. Later, the Tuscarora joined the confederacy.

Wampum belts were made from strings of shell beads.

This is a Wampum belt. The designs of Wampum belts recorded important agreements and events.

Today, the Confederacy chiefs still meet to make laws and decide on **customs**.

Mohawk children at a pow-wow.

Iroquois tribes still get together at **pow-wows** and festivals. These Mohawk children are taking part in a **smoke dance** competition.

Iroquois culture

The Iroquois believe that life began when Skywoman fell from the sky.

Skywoman landed on a turtle's back which grew to become TURTLE ISLAND, the Iroquois name for America.

LACROSSE is the best known Iroquois game. Players threw a ball, and used a net on a stick to catch it. Sometimes tribes played lacrosse instead of having a war!

Villagers of the southeast

The Cherokee were SKILFUL FARMERS who grew crops in the rich, dark soil of the southeast. They settled in small villages along rivers and streams.

Cherokee families often had two houses. A rectangular house made from wood and grass, for the summer, and a cone-shaped winter house covered with clay or woven mats, for warmth.

Summer house

Winter house

A reconstruction of traditional Cherokee homes.

Cherokee women worked in the fields and made clothes from deerskin. Cherokee men hunted for deer and bears with bows and arrows.

The Cherokee grew corn, beans, squash and tobacco. Corn could not be eaten until the yearly *Green Corn Ceremony*. This great festival was celebrated in the autumn after the last crop had ripened.

A Cherokee man wears traditional clothing during a ceremonial dance.

Cherokee artefacts

During the **GREEN CORN CEREMONY**, men danced and shook **gourd** rattles to thank the spirits for a bountiful harvest.

Tribal leaders smoked tobacco in **CLAY PIPES** during important ceremonial events.

This emerald **AMULET**, or lucky charm, was worn by a Cherokee chief.

The trail of tears

In the early 1800s, **non-Indian settlers** began to want the Cherokee's farmland for themselves. In 1838, the **US government** made 15,000 Cherokee give up their land and leave their homes.

The Cherokee people were forced to march west to what was called **Indian Territory.** During the journey, they were guarded by US soldiers and by Indians who were working for the US government.

Thousands of Cherokee people died of disease and starvation on the long march. The journey is known as *The Trail of Tears*.

This painting by Robert Lindneux is called "The Trail of Tears".

Some Cherokee refused to leave. They hid out in the mountains.

Cherokee history

A Cherokee man, named SEQUOYA, made up an alphabet so his people could write down their spoken language.

The alphabet turned all the different Cherokee sounds into just 85 characters.

In 1828, the Cherokee published the first Native American newspaper, called the CHEROKEE PHOENIX.

Buffalo hunters

A sea of grass grew on America's Great Plains. Many grazing animals fed on the grass, especially BUFFALO. To the Sioux, the buffalo was the most honoured and respected of all the creatures on the plains.

American buffalo

Every year, large herds of buffalo **migrated** across the plains.

The Sioux relied on the buffalo for food, and for **hides** to make clothes and **tipis**. So, when the buffalo moved, the Sioux followed.

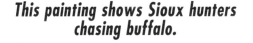

This painting shows Sioux hunters chasing buffalo.

Sioux horses could outrun buffalo. They were trained to run close alongside the mighty animals, so the hunter could shoot an arrow or throw a spear into the buffalo's neck.

Hunters and warriors

Great Plains Indians performed ceremonies and **rituals** before and after buffalo hunts.

APPALOOSAS are horses with a short, fast stride. They are bred by the Indians.

Warriors held their **HIDE SHIELDS** in one hand, when on horseback. The shields protected them against enemy arrows.

Life on the Plains

The Sioux lived in CONE-SHAPED TENTS called **tipis**. These portable houses were just right for their **nomadic** lifestyle. Tipis were covered with buffalo **hides** and had frames made from large, wooden poles.

A Sioux dancer in ceremonial clothes stands beside a tipi.

Buffalo herds moved quickly, and Sioux families had to be ready to follow. Women could take down a tipi in just fifteen minutes.

18

When moving from place to place, Sioux men made a travois, or carrier, by attaching the narrow ends of tipi poles to the back of a horse.

This photograph shows Sioux children riding on a travois.

Whole villages moved several times during a single season of buffalo hunting. When making camp, Sioux families arranged their tipis in a circle.

This painting shows Sioux families in a tipi village.

Sioux artefacts

In battle, Sioux warriors would try to get close enough to touch an enemy, but not kill him! This was called COUNTING COUP.

Warriors used coup sticks to touch their enemies.

These Sioux MOCCASINS were made from buffalo hide. They are decorated with porcupine quills.

People of the Mesas

The Hopi have lived in the deserts of the southwest for THOUSANDS of years. Hopi people still live in northern Arizona today. They live on top of three flat, tabletop hills with steep sides. The hills are called mesas.

This picture shows the Hopi mesa village of Walpi.

One mesa village, Oraibi, is a thousand years old. In ancient times, the mesas were natural protection against enemy attack.

Hopi houses are made out of sandstone and adobe, sun-dried clay.

Hopi houses are built one on top of another.

The houses are stacked one on top of another, with the roof of one house serving as a terrace for the one above. Ladders make it easy to climb from house to house.

Hopi myths and legends

These stone drawings show **TAWA** the Sun God and **SPIDER WOMAN**.

In the beginning of time, they sang a magic song and formed animals, birds and insects. Then they shaped men and women and placed them all on the earth.

This stone drawing shows **KOKOPELI**, the mythical, humpback flute player. Kokopeli plays and dances when people are sad.

Desert farmers

Maize has been important to Hopi life for thousands of years. It grows well in the HOT, DESERT CLIMATE. Hopi men also grow gardens of beans, squash and pumpkins.

This Hopi farmer is growing maize in the dry desert.

To grow crops you need rain. The **Kachinas** are **spirits** who help to make it rain.

The Hopi hold special ceremonies where performers in beautiful costumes sing and dance for rain.

At some ceremonies dancers perform as Kachina spirits who call the clouds over the fields of maize. Some ceremonies include dancing with live rattlesnakes.

This is a wooden Kachina doll.

Hopi artists carve wooden Kachina dolls. They are given to Hopi girls at Kachina ceremonies.

Hopi life and customs

Maize roots can reach twenty feet underground, helping the plant find water in the dry sand.

Gourds are grown to make rattles, cups, scrapers and containers.

Young Hopi women wore their hair in two rolls, called BUTTERFLY WHORLS, until they got married.

23

Glossary

CLAN A group of people related by blood.

CRADLEBOARDS Flat pieces of wood used for carrying babies. The mother carries the cradleboard on her back.

CULTURE The way of life and the beliefs of a group of people.

CUSTOMS Things that are done in a particular way again and again. They are handed down from one generation to the next.

ENVIRONMENT The place where a person lives and the things that affect that place, such as the weather or type of land.

GOURD A hard-skinned vegetable.

HIDES Animal skins.

INDIAN TERRITORY The part of North America that is now Oklahoma.

KACHINAS (Katchinas) Hopi rain spirits.

LEGENDS Tales about supernatural creatures or events.

MIGRATED Moved from one area to another. Animals migrate to a new place to find more food or to breed.

NOMADIC People who move from place to place with their homes.

NON-INDIAN SETTLERS Settlers who came from Europe and claimed for themselves the lands where Indians had lived for thousands of years.

ORIGIN STORIES Tales that explain how a group of people came to be.

POW-WOW A modern-day festival where members of many tribes meet up.

RITUALS Religious or important ceremonies where certain actions are carried out in a set order.

SMOKE DANCE A dance said to imitate the way in which dancers fanned smoke from the longhouse fires, out through the holes in the roof.

SPIRITS Unexplained forces in nature, like those that control the weather; a life-like force within living things.

STORYTELLERS People who tell stories that keep tribal traditions alive. They teach the history of the land, and show the proper way for humans to live together.

TERRITORY The area across the upper part of New York State.

TIPIS Portable cone-shaped tents covered with buffalo hides

TRADITIONS Beliefs, actions or ways of doing something that are handed down from one generation to the next.

US GOVERNMENT Within a hundred years of arriving in America the non-indian settlers organised themselves into colonies. In 1776, the settlers formed the government of the United States. The new government made laws which the Indians had to live by.

Index